LET'S MAKE HIST[ORY]

The Middle Ages

Paul Titley

Illustrations by Ken Petts
Models and diagrams by Hilary Evans

OWLET BOOKS
London · Sydney · Toronto

SIEGE TOWERS

One way of attacking high castle walls was to use siege towers. These towers were made of wood and consisted of a number of platforms. As the picture shows, the attacking soldiers climbed from platform to platform on movable ladders.

Siege towers were built on wheels so that they could be pushed right up to the walls. The top of each tower was protected by a roof. The whole tower was usually covered with wet animal hides as a protection against fire arrows. Some towers had a small drawbridge at the top, and a few also had a battering ram at the base.

Siege towers took weeks to construct. While the carpenters were building the towers, soldiers would work under cover of darkness filling in the castle moat.

How to make the siege tower

Materials: shoe box and lid, 4 thread reels, brown paper, string, 2 wooden rods, pencil, scissors, ruler, glue, craft knife, paint, paintbrush

Cut shoe box lid into 3. Cut 3cm squares in corners of middle and 1 end section.

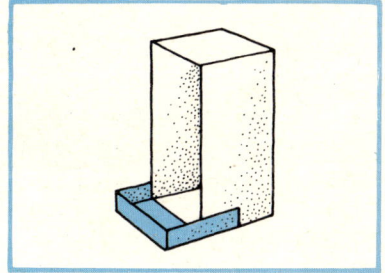

Glue other end section onto box as base of siege tower.

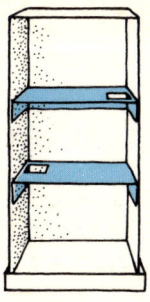

Glue lid sections into box as platforms. Make top platform from end section.

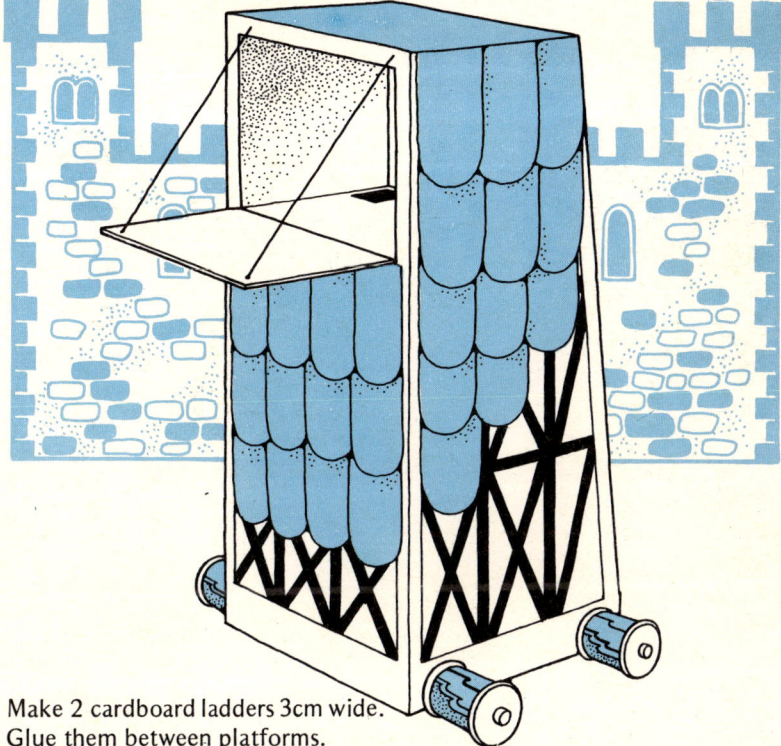

Make 2 cardboard ladders 3cm wide. Glue them between platforms.

Cut drawbridge in tower front. Thread string from drawbridge to top of tower.

Cut and glue 2 cardboard triangles to tower sides.

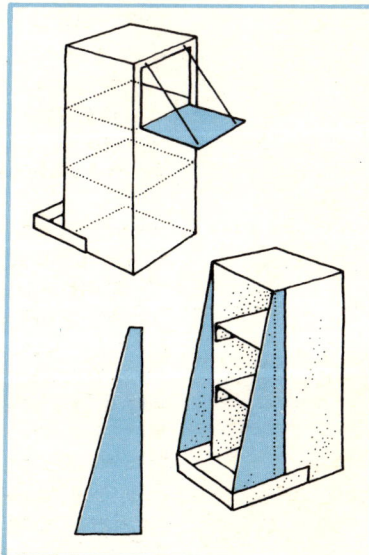

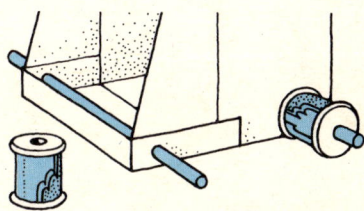

Make 2 holes in each side at tower base. Push 2 wooden rods through holes to form axles. Glue 4 thread reels to rods for wheels.

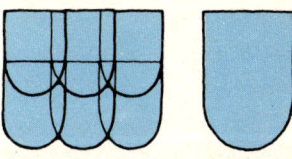

Colour siege tower and paint beams. Cut some brown paper shapes 7 x 5cm for animal hides. Glue them onto tower sides and front so that they overlap each other.

A CARRIAGE

During the Middle Ages some of the old Roman roads were passable, but most other roads were in a dreadful state. Travelling, particularly in winter, was difficult. People who could afford to travel by horseback did so. There were also some carriages, used mainly by noble ladies.

The carriages had to be strong. They had a base of planks, thick axles, and four spoked wheels. The sides were panelled in wood. The top, which was brightly coloured, was probably made of painted canvas stretched over iron hoops. It would have taken a team of four horses to pull such a carriage.

The carriages had no springs, so they must have been uncomfortable to ride in. The ladies probably reclined on cushions to make the journey pleasanter.

How to make the carriage

Materials: cardboard box, 1m wooden dowel, 4 circular lids 11cm diameter, cartridge paper, cardboard, 4 drawing pins, pencil, ruler, scissors, glue, craft knife, felt-tip pens, paint, paintbrush

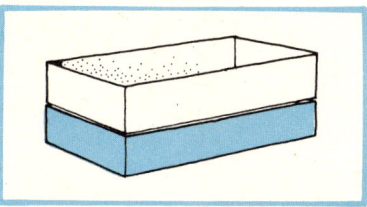

Cut sides of small cardboard box 32 x 16cm down to 7cm deep.

Cut two 20cm lengths of dowel for axles. Attach them to box base 4cm from each end with strips of cardboard.

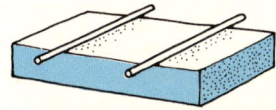

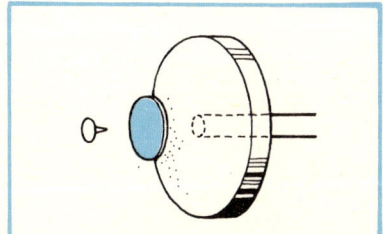

Fit wheels onto cart. Glue a cardboard circle 3cm in diameter in centre of each wheel. Push drawing pins through circles into axles.

Glue paper top into carriage. Cut narrow cardboard strips and glue them over each end.

Cut four 3cm cardboard squares. Glue them centrally inside circular boxes. Make holes for axles.

Cut piece of cartridge paper 42 x 32 cm for curved top. Leaving 7cm margins top and bottom, draw pattern using felt-tip pen.

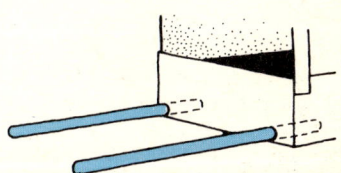

Cut 2 dowel shafts 26cm long. Make 2 holes in front of carriage and glue shafts in position.

Paint wheels and cardboard parts of carriage.

5

POLE ARMS

Pole arms were developed from farm implements, such as forks and scythes, with which peasants defended themselves. As the name suggests, a pole arm had a long wooden shaft. It was usually between 1.5 and 2 metres long, and so a person needed considerable strength to hold and use it.

There were various types of pole arms. Among the most effective were the bills made by the Italians and Swiss. The picture shows a typical bill head. It had a spike for thrusting, a sharp axe blade for slashing, and a spear-like fluke at the top. It was, therefore, three weapons in one. Because steel was very expensive bill heads were usually made of iron, and then had a steel edge hammered onto the blade.

How to make the pole arm

Materials: thick and thin cardboard, 1.5m garden cane, kitchen foil, glue, pencil, ruler, scissors, craft knife, paint, paintbrush

Cut billhead from rectangle of thick cardboard 38 x 22cm. Paint both sides grey.

Glue folded strip of kitchen foil 4cm wide over blade edge.

Cut rectangle of thin cardboard 26 x 20cm. Spread glue over one side. Roll cardboard tightly into tube that will fit over top of cane.

Make 2 cuts 12cm long down sides of tube.

Flatten the 2 sides and cut tops into shape shown. Paint tube grey.

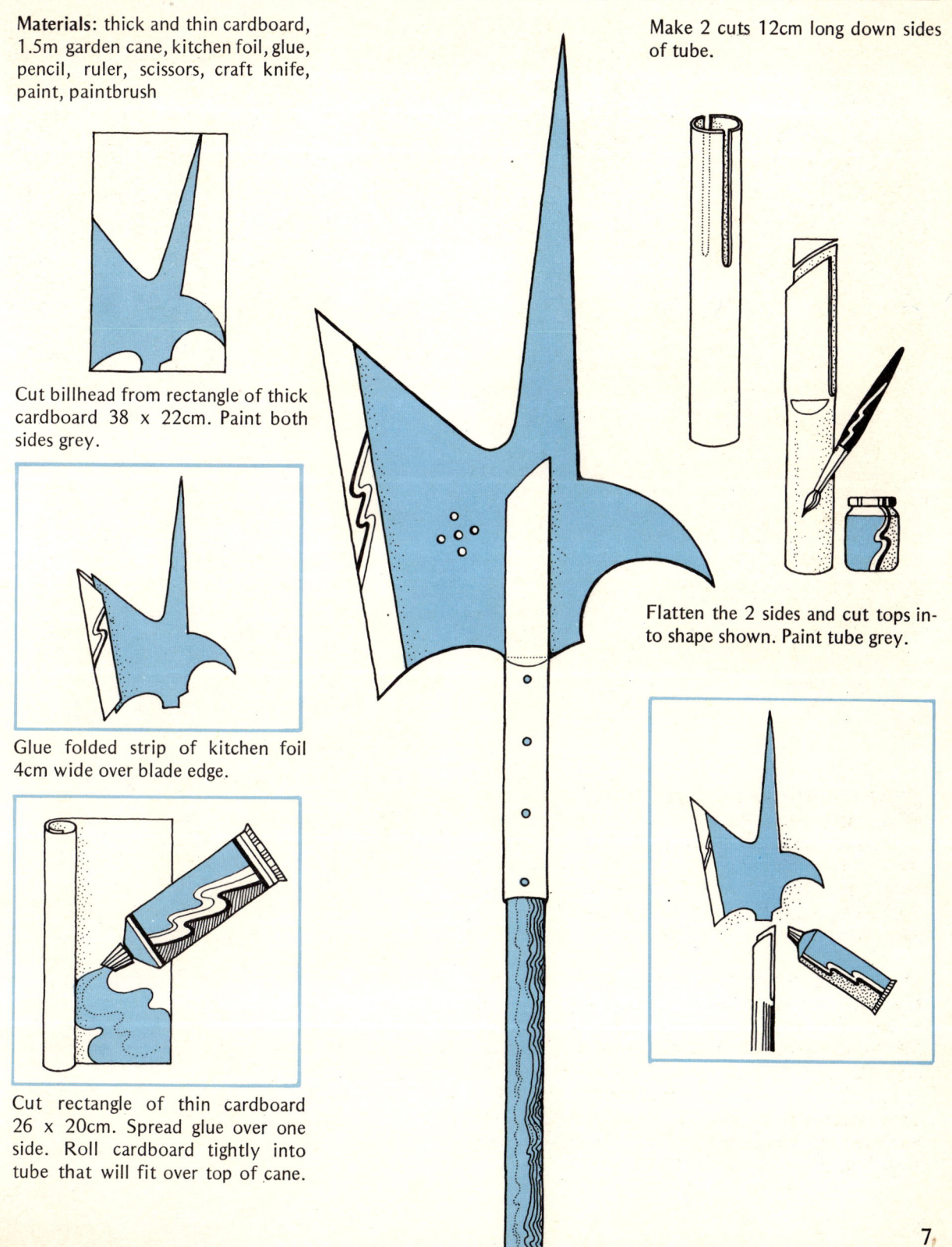

A MOTTE AND BAILEY CASTLE

The earliest castles were motte and bailey castles. The motte was a large mound flattened at the top. Where possible, natural rock formations were used, but many mottes were man-made. The tower, called a keep, was built on the motte. At first, keeps were made of timber and surrounded by a wooden palisade.

The bailey was the courtyard at the base of the motte. It was encircled by a moat and a timber palisade. The barns, servants' and soldiers' quarters, and sometimes the lord's hall were in the bailey, for the keep was used as the last place of defence.

Attackers had to cross the moat first, seize the

bailey, and then try to storm the keep. Clearly, defenders on the motte had great advantages over people trying to fight their way up.

Motte and bailey castles were later strengthened by replacing the timber palisades and keep with stone walls and a stone tower. The only entrance to the bailey was a gatehouse protected by a portcullis, and a drawbridge was the only way over the moat. Stone defences were more difficult to batter down and could not be set on fire.

How to make the castle

Materials: cardboard, newspaper, wallpaper paste, matchboxes, matches with heads removed, balsa cement, craft knife, ruler, pencil, paint, paintbrush

Draw 2 circles on cardboard rectangle 28 x 48cm.

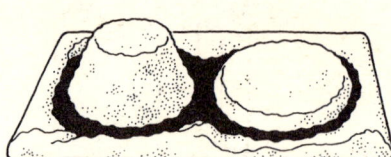

Build up sides of rectangle with screwed up newspaper and strips, leaving ditch all round motte and bailey.

Hold matches against bridge and mark with pencil. Cut to size and glue in place. Make 6 struts for long bridge and 4 struts for short one.

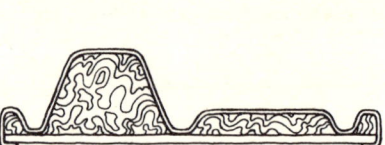

While model is drying put saucer on motte and plate on bailey to keep tops flat. When dry, paint model.

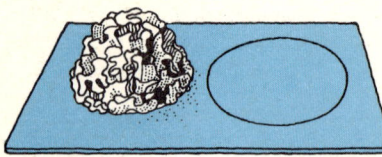

Screw up pieces of newspaper and glue them inside small circle to form motte. Glue several layers of newspaper over motte, making neat mound about 8cm high.

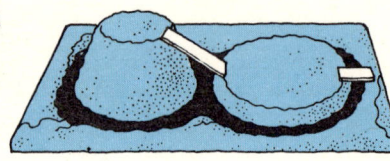

Cut 2 cardboard strips 1.5cm wide for bridges. Glue matches along edges on underside of strips. Paint bridges and glue them to model.

Cut many matches 2.5cm long and point one end. Glue matches around motte and bailey to form palisades. Leave gaps of about 3cm at bridges for gate arches. Build matchstick palisade on each side of long bridge to join motte to bailey.

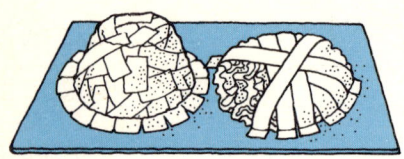

Similarly, make bailey 2cm high inside large circle.

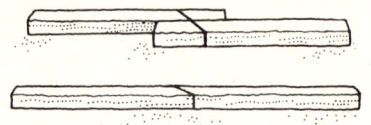

Use matches for struts to support bridges. If 1 match is too short, cut 2 diagonally and glue together.

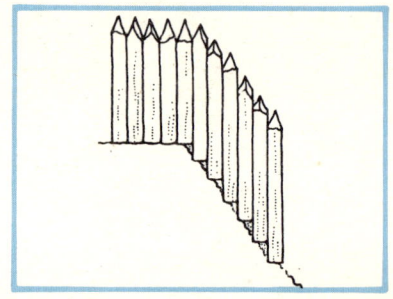

Use longer matchsticks down sloping sides of motte.

Make 3 gate arches from matches about 3.3cm long glued together in pairs. Make arches individually to fit gaps in palisades.

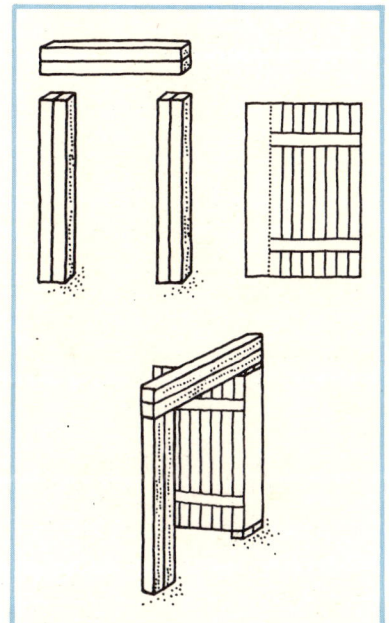

Cut 3 cardboard gates with flaps. Paint them and glue to arches. Glue gate arches to model.

Glue 2 small matchboxes together vertically to make keep. Cut rectangle of thin cardboard with 2 triangular gables. Glue this around matchboxes. Cut cardboard rectangle for roof. Score along centre, fold into shape, and glue in place.

Make buildings for bailey from small matchboxes glued together horizontally. Cut 2 thin cardboard rectangles to cover boxes. Make triangular gables of 1 rectangle higher than the other. This will make a taller building. Cut 2 cardboard rectangles for the roof. Score, fold and glue in place.

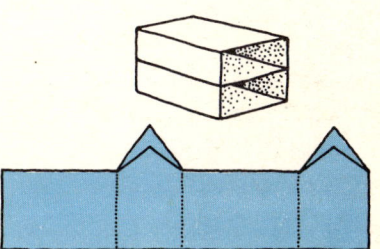

Paint buildings and glue them onto the model.

11

A CROSSBOW

The crossbow was a powerful weapon. Its bolts or arrows could pierce chainmail. The main parts of the crossbow were the bow made of sinew, horn and wood, and the wooden shoulder stock.

Crossbows took considerable strength to load. The crossbowman put his foot in the foot stirrup and hooked the bowstring to a hook fastened to his belt. This gave him the leverage to draw the string back until it was taut. Then he loaded the bolt or arrow into the groove in the stock, and fired it by releasing the trigger mechanism.

The main disadvantage of crossbows was the time taken to load them. By the 15th century the English longbow, which could be loaded and fired much more quickly, was accepted as a superior weapon.

How to make the crossbow

Materials: wooden lath, stick, balsa wood 3mm thick, large rubber band, drawing pins, pencil, ruler, craft knife, balsa cement

Cut 2 balsa wood rectangles 4 x 7cm. Cut circles in middle of these pieces 1cm from top, and glue to stock. Thread crosspiece through holes.

Cut 2 trigger pieces from strips of balsa wood 1.2cm wide. Use drawing pins to fix them onto end of stock. Lower B to lock trigger.

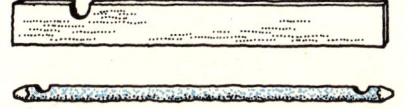

Cut 4mm thick wooden lath 34 x 3cm for stock. Make groove 3cm from end for crosspiece. Cut stick to 34cm and cut a notch at each end.

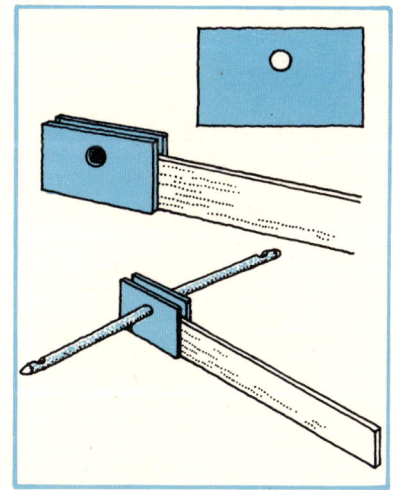

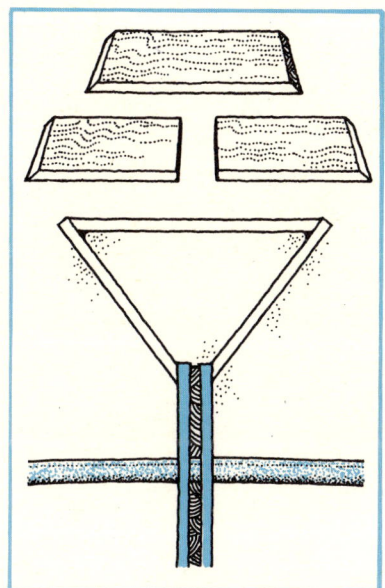

Cut 2 balsa wood rectangles 3 x 7cm, and 1 rectangle 3 x 9cm. Shape edges and glue pieces onto front of bow.

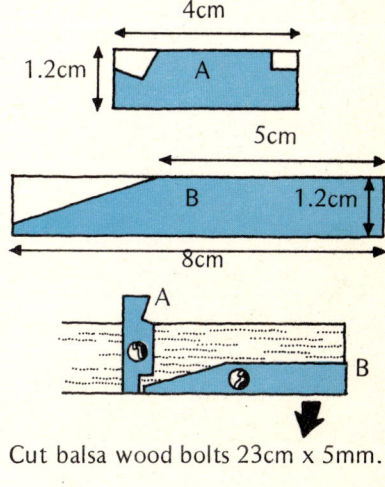

Cut balsa wood bolts 23cm x 5mm.

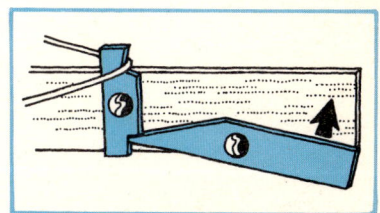

Cut rubber band and tie ends around notches in crosspiece. Fit a bolt onto crossbow. Slip rubber band over trigger A. Lift B to fire.

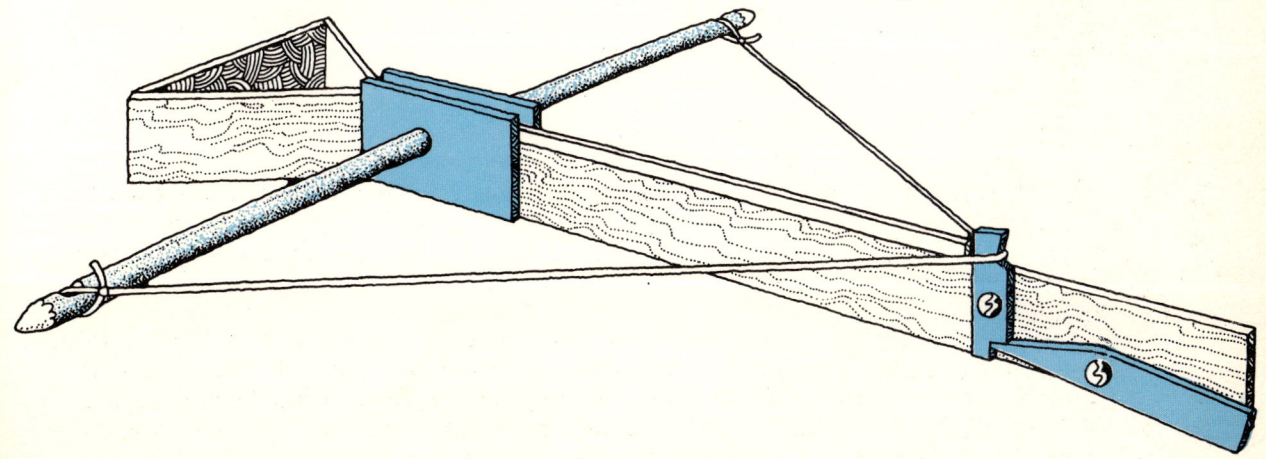

13

A KNIGHT'S HELMET

To make a helmet the armourer used a special anvil shaped like a man's head. He heated the metal and beat it around the anvil until he had the shape and thickness required. Making an ordinary helmet was not particularly difficult, but in the Middle Ages the protective visor, which could be pulled down over the face, was introduced. The visor had to have eye slits cut into it. Then it had to be fitted onto the helmet in such a way as to allow it to be raised above the helmet and yet not fall too far forward, leaving the knight's face exposed.

Helmets were always worn over a round padded hat, not directly on the head.

How to make the helmet

Materials: cardboard, newspaper, glue, wallpaper paste, paper fasteners, ruler, scissors, paint, paintbrush

Make a large cardboard tube that will fit over your head.

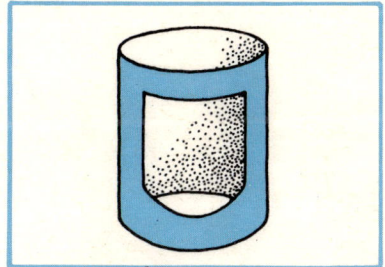

Cut away the front part.

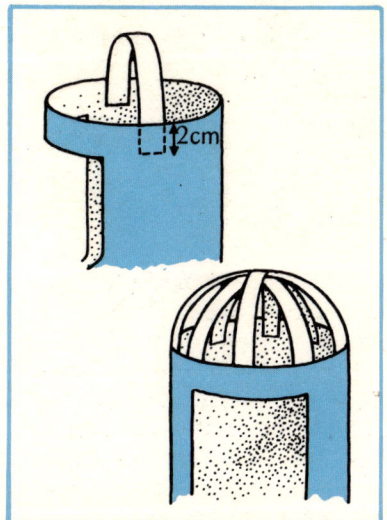

Cut 4 cardboard strips for curved helmet top. Make them 2cm wide and as long as ½ the helmet circumference plus 4cm. Glue strips onto inside of helmet.

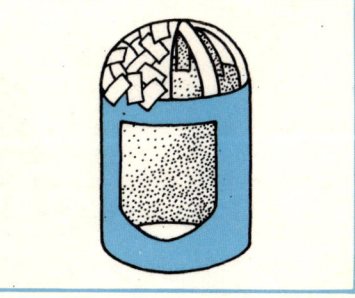

Tear strips of newspaper. Using wallpaper paste, glue 4 or more layers of strips over cardboard frame.

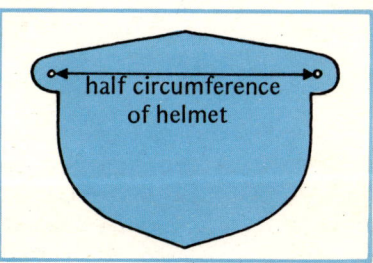

Make cardboard visor ½ helmet circumference plus 4cm wide, and as tall as tube part of helmet plus 3cm.

Cut 2 slits for eyes. Paint helmet and visor silver. Paint a black cross and ventilation holes on visor.

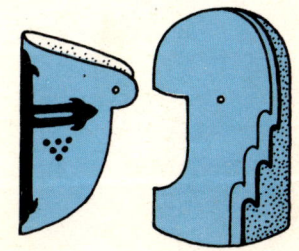

Make 2 holes on opposite sides of helmet. Attach visor to helmet with paper fasteners. Open fasteners on inside of helmet.

15

A SHIELD

Shields varied in design and size during the Middle Ages. The picture shows one of the commonest shapes. This shield was not very large, about 35 centimetres wide and 50 centimetres long, and came to a neat point at the base. It was made of wood covered with canvas and leather. Some shields were flat, others were convex. The knight held the shield by an iron grip at the back.

When knights began to wear helmets that covered their faces it was necessary to have some way of identifying them. Therefore, the knight had his coat of arms, called heraldry, painted on the surface of his shield, which is called 'the field'. Each coat of arms was different. Some were quite simple, with little more than a cross or bar, but others were highly decorated with pictures of plants and animals.

How to make the shield

Materials: strong cardboard, tracing paper, glue, pencil, ruler, scissors, paint, paintbrush

Cut a rectangle of strong cardboard 50 x 35cm. Draw a line down centre of rectangle.

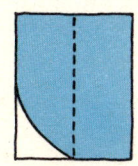 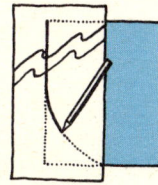

Draw curved side of shield in one half of rectangle. Place a sheet of tracing paper over this half. Trace curved line with soft pencil.

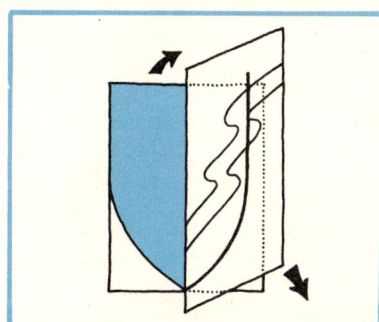

Turn tracing paper face down on other half of rectangle. Draw over curved line so that it shows on cardboard.

Cut out shield shape. Carefully paint a design on front.

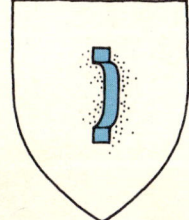

Cut strip of cardboard for grip. It must be long enough to fit around your arm. Glue grip to back of shield.

17

WOMEN'S HATS

During the Middle Ages fashions in head-dress changed frequently. The years between 1370 and 1450 saw some extraordinary shapes in hats. These hats completely hid a woman's hair. In fact, not only did women have their hair cut short, but some even had the hair on their necks plucked out.

One style of hat had a very high point with a velvet roll at the front decorated with jewels. The point was covered with gold or silver tissue, or beautiful brocade. A fine veil hung from the top of the point down the wearer's back, and a stiffened veil partly hid the face. Hats like these must have been very uncomfortable to wear.

How to make the hat

Materials: coloured and tracing paper, old pair of tights, lightweight scarf, paper handkerchiefs, buttons, sequins or beads, sticky tape, pencil, glue, ruler, scissors

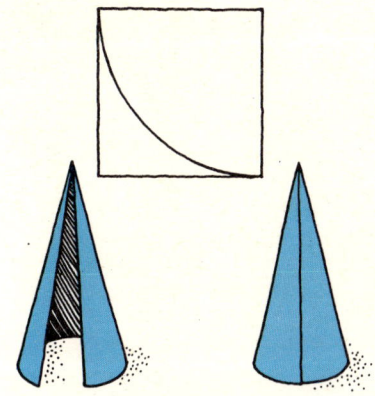

On large sheet of coloured paper draw quarter circle with 50cm radius. Cut out shape and fold into cone that will fit on your head. Glue down edges.

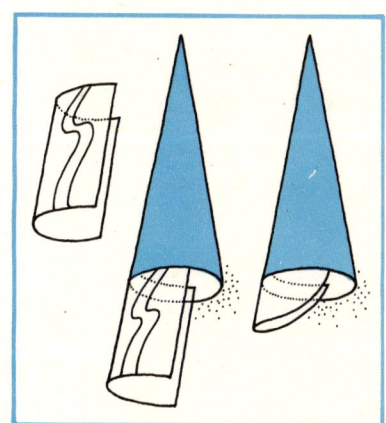

Glue a sheet of tracing paper about 40cm long inside paper cone. Cut it to form veil.

Cut 1 leg from old pair of tights. Fill it with paper handkerchiefs to make a long roll. Knot ends together when it is long enough to fit round cone base.

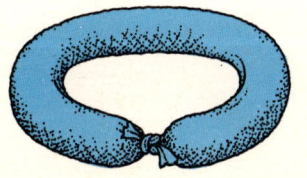

Cover roll ends with paper rectangle. Decorate it with paper strips, beads, buttons, etc. Glue roll to cone.

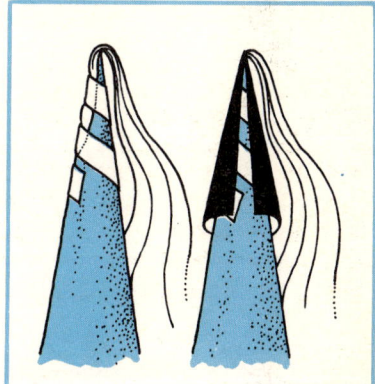

Use sticky tape to fix corner of scarf to hat. Cut small quarter circle of coloured paper and glue it onto hat to cover sticky tape.

19

AN ALTAR CROSS

The Middle Ages were a time of great religious faith. Medieval churches and cathedrals were among the finest buildings in Europe, and many of the treasures made for them were magnificent. The French goldsmiths of Lorraine were particularly skilled craftsmen. This 12th century altar cross is an example of their work.

The base of the cross was beaten out of gold and highly decorated. It was raised on four beautifully carved feet. Enamelled pictures of the apostles Matthew, Mark, Luke and John were set in the gold base. The cross and the figure of Christ were also made of solid gold. Crosses like this are among the most valuable religious treasures.

How to make the cross

Materials: plastic carton, cardboard, paper, modelling clay, pencil, ruler, scissors, glue, paint, paintbrush

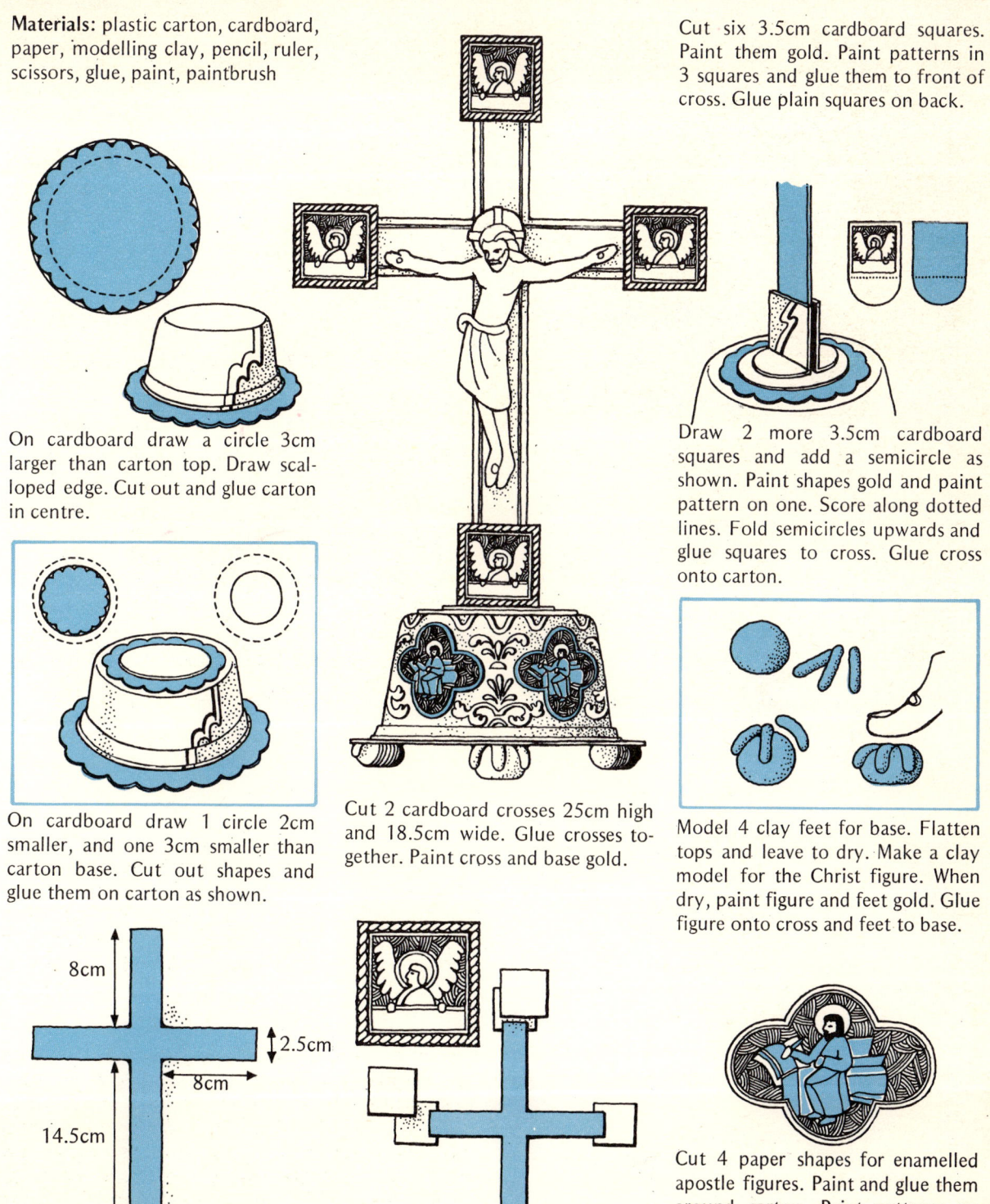

On cardboard draw a circle 3cm larger than carton top. Draw scalloped edge. Cut out and glue carton in centre.

On cardboard draw 1 circle 2cm smaller, and one 3cm smaller than carton base. Cut out shapes and glue them on carton as shown.

Cut 2 cardboard crosses 25cm high and 18.5cm wide. Glue crosses together. Paint cross and base gold.

Cut six 3.5cm cardboard squares. Paint them gold. Paint patterns in 3 squares and glue them to front of cross. Glue plain squares on back.

Draw 2 more 3.5cm cardboard squares and add a semicircle as shown. Paint shapes gold and paint pattern on one. Score along dotted lines. Fold semicircles upwards and glue squares to cross. Glue cross onto carton.

Model 4 clay feet for base. Flatten tops and leave to dry. Make a clay model for the Christ figure. When dry, paint figure and feet gold. Glue figure onto cross and feet to base.

Cut 4 paper shapes for enamelled apostle figures. Paint and glue them around carton. Paint patterns on carton.

21

A CANDLESTICK

There were two common types of candlestick in the Middle Ages, a cup to hold the candle, and a spike, or pricket, that pierced the base of the candle. Even the pricket candlesticks used in the homes of fairly well-to-do people were of a simple design. They were raised on three iron legs, and had a metal rim below the spike to catch the dripping fat or wax. Candlesticks like these could be made by the village blacksmith.

Church altars usually had a pair of candlesticks, one on each side of the cross. They were often the work of highly skilled goldsmiths or silversmiths, and were very elaborate. Although most were only plated with precious metal, some, particularly those in the great cathedrals, were made of solid gold.

How to make the candlestick

Materials: 2 sweets tubes, circular plastic lid, eggbox, cardboard, ruler, pencil, scissors, glue, paint, brush

Cut 14cm cardboard square. Draw 4cm square in middle. Draw in diagonals. Cut away shaded triangle. Cut diagonals of inner square.

Score all lines and fold into triangular base shape. Glue down flaps on top.

Cut 3 cardboard legs. Score down centre and fold. Glue legs on inside of triangular base.

Glue 2 sweets tubes together for stem. Cut 2 cups from soft plastic or cardboard eggbox. If necessary, enlarge holes in sides. Glue cups onto stem. Cover any holes in cups with paper.

Make small hole in middle of lid. Push a short pencil through hole. Glue lid onto tube. Glue tube to base. Paint candlestick gold. Paint on patterns.

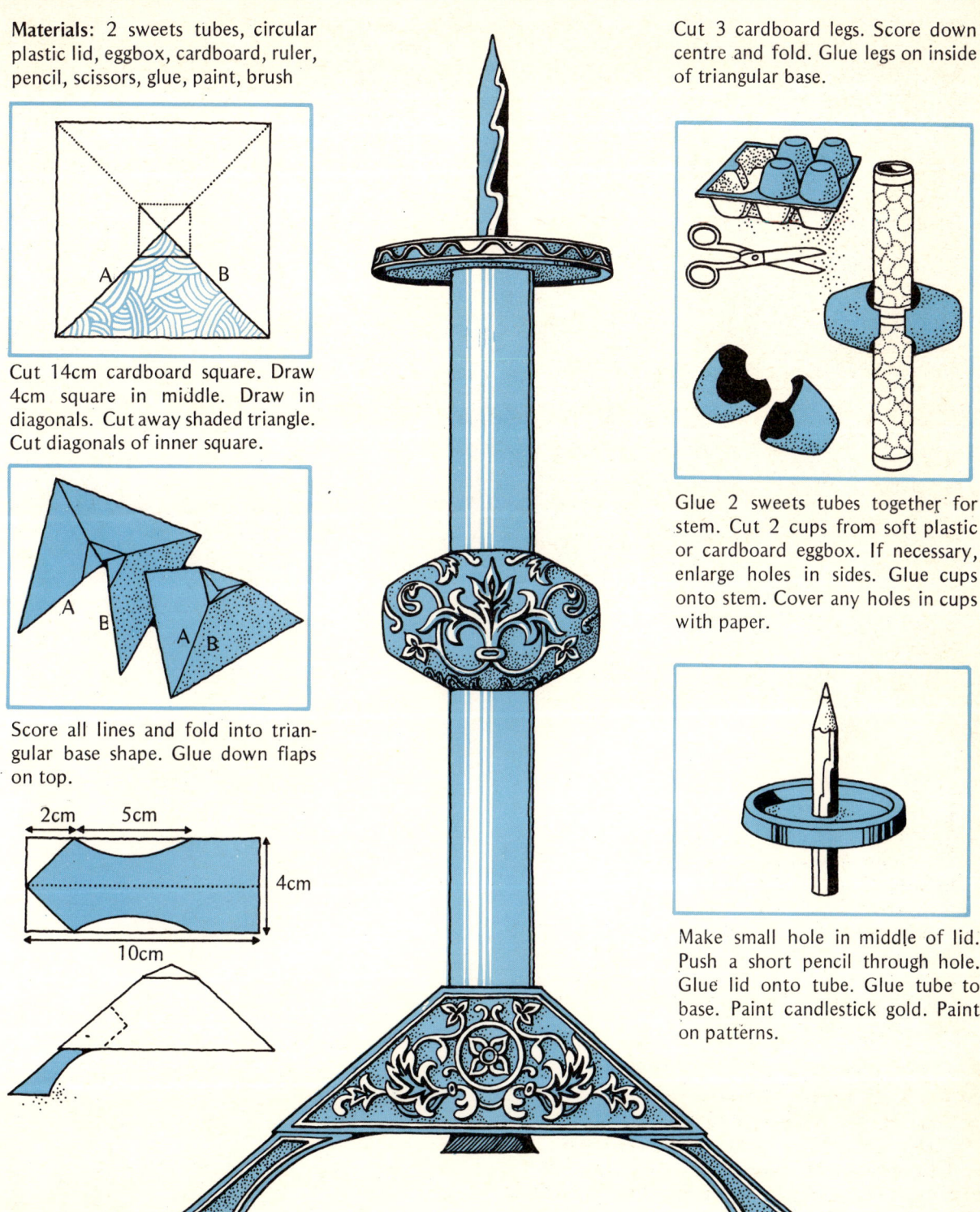

A LUTE

The lute was one of the most popular musical instruments in the Middle Ages. It had a pear-shaped body, a fairly short neck, and a pegboard that went off at a sharp angle to the neck. It was designed in this way to counteract the heavy pull of the strings when they were being tuned.

The neck was made of a number of staves glued together, and this, plus raising the strings on frets, added to the resonance. The strings were attached to rollers in the pegboard so that they could be tightened and slackened to get the right note. At first most lutes had five strings. Later the number rose to eleven, and by the 17th century some lutes had twenty-six.

Lutes gave a gentle sound, rather like a soft harp, and were ideal for accompanying singers.

How to make the lute

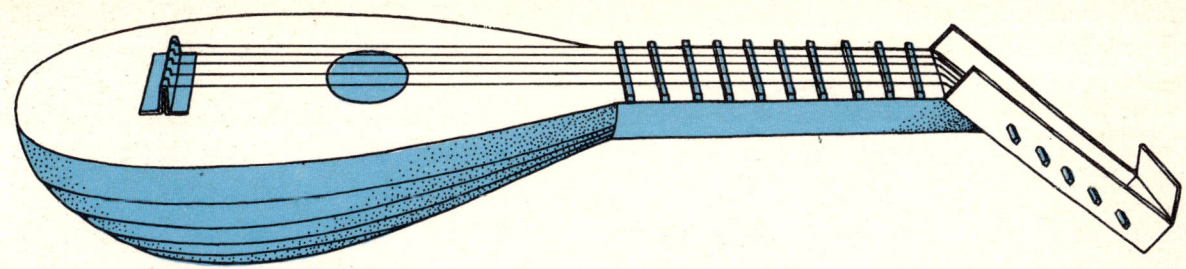

Materials: cardboard, cardboard tube 4cm diameter, stiff brown paper, nylon thread, matches, pencil, ruler, glue, scissors, paint, paintbrush

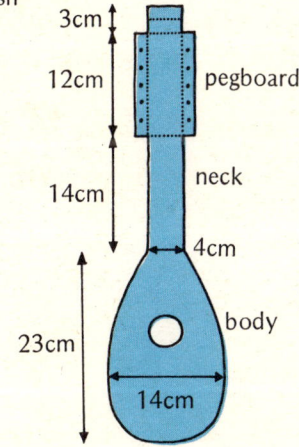

Cut lute shape from cardboard. Score dotted lines. Cut 1 hole in body and 5 small holes in each side of pegboard for matches.

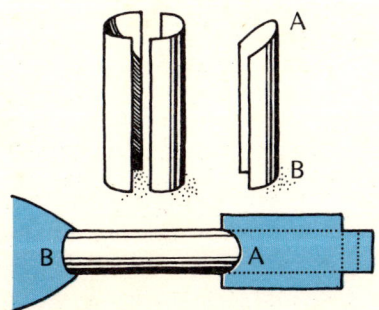

Cut cardboard tube to 17cm. Cut it in half lengthways. Discard one half; shape top of other and glue it to back of lute as shown.

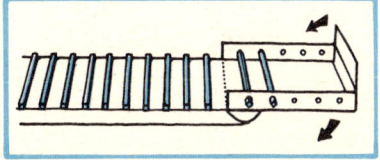

Turn lute over. Glue 10 matches on neck for frets. Fold up sides and end of pegboard and glue them together. Fold pegboard down and glue to tube. Thread 5 matches through holes in pegboard sides.

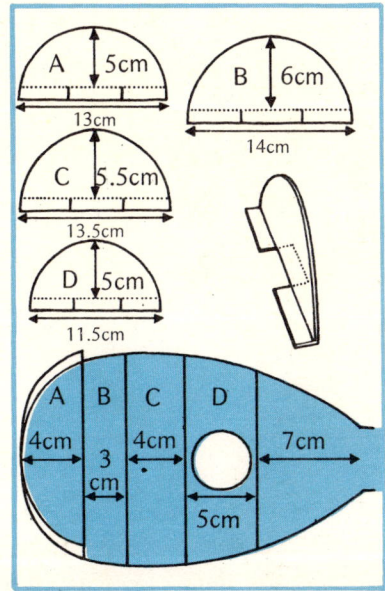

Cut cardboard shapes A, B, C, D. Score dotted lines. Fold flaps alternately backwards and forwards. Glue shapes to back of lute. Glue cardboard strip at bottom.

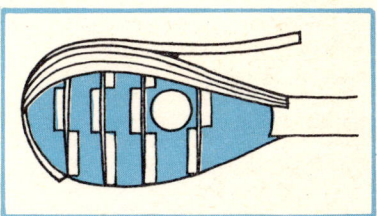

Cut some paper strips 36 x 2cm. Glue a strip from neck to bottom of lute. Trim end. Glue on another strip, overlapping first. Cover lute body in this way.

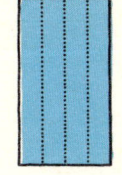 

Cut cardboard rectangle 7 x 4cm. Score dotted lines and fold to form bridge. Make 5 cuts in top. Glue bridge onto lute body. Paint all cardboard parts.

Cut 5 nylon strings. Knot ends and slip into cuts in bridge. Tie other ends onto matches on pegboard.

25

A MEDIEVAL CHAIR

Chairs were rare in the Middle Ages and were used only by important people. The chair was a symbol of authority, which is why today the person presiding over a meeting is called a chairman or chairperson.

The ornate chair shown here was made by Italian craftsmen, and was clearly developed from the humble three-legged stool. The curved pieces could have been made in one of two ways. Most probably a branch that had grown in this shape was chosen or, if not, a thin lath was bent after being heated with steam. Either way, the curved back was made in two sections. The intricate patterns on the front would have been carved by skilled woodworkers. When the pieces were ready, they were fitted together with mortise and tenon joints.

How to make the chair

Materials: 2 plastic cartons, pencil, cardboard, scissors, glue, paint, paintbrush

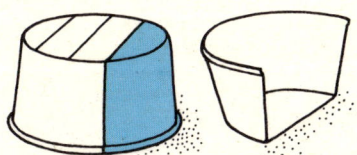

Cut a ¼ section from each carton.

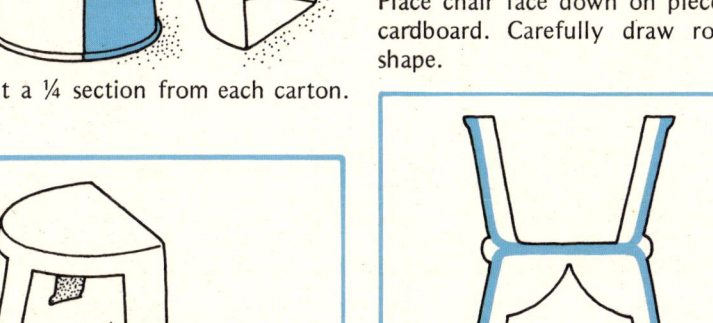

Place chair face down on piece of cardboard. Carefully draw round shape.

Using outline, draw front of chair. Make arms and legs about 1cm wide. Cut out cardboard shape and glue to chair front.

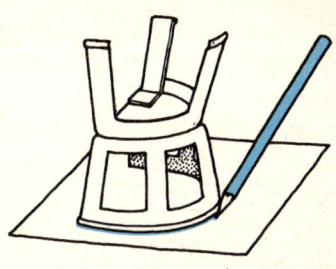

Turn chair upside down on piece of cardboard. Draw round top of chair.

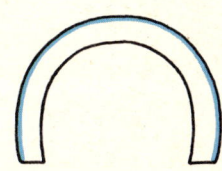

Using outline, draw top of chair about 1cm wide. Cut out shape and glue to chair. Paint chair. Paint on patterned carving.

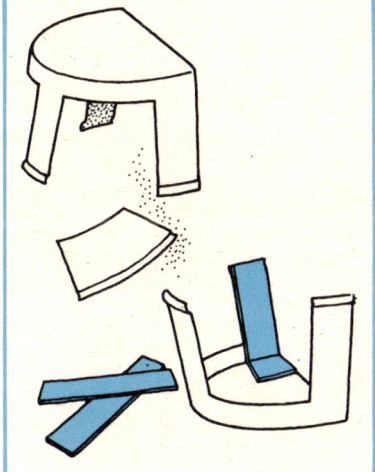

Cut away 2 sections from 1 carton to make 3 legs about 2.5cm wide. Glue strips of cardboard to legs to strengthen them.

Make top of chair from other carton. Cut away 4 sections, leaving 5 supports about 2cm wide. Glue cartons together.

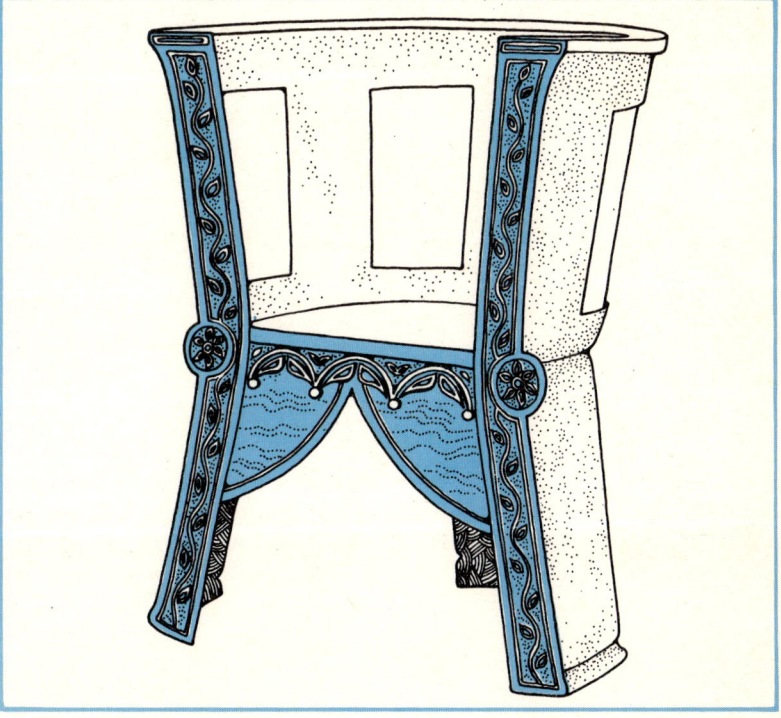

27

A MERCHANT'S STRONGBOX

There were no banks in the Middle Ages, so wealthy merchants had to look after their own money and valuables. They usually had a strongbox made of wood bound with iron and covered with leather. Although many of these strongboxes were attractively decorated, their main function was security.

The box was made of strong oak planks. Skilled carpenters were expected to fit the lid flush to the chest so that it couldn't be prised open. Locksmiths were employed to make the strongbox as secure as possible. Some boxes had three locks. The middle lock was built into the chest and had a very complicated mechanism. The other two were not built in, but they were extremely heavy, and their hinges, clasps, and staples were far too powerful to be forced off.

How to make the strongbox

Materials: shoe box, covered corrugated cardboard, plastic bottle, grey paper, split peas, glue, scissors, ruler, pencil, craft knife, paint, paintbrush

Cut 2 covered corrugated cardboard rectangles to fit inside box at back and front, adding 1cm top and bottom.

Score along the 1cm lines. Fold 1cm sections over and glue down. Glue rectangles into box. Make 2 more for box ends.

Cut top and base off plastic bottle. Cut middle section into strips.

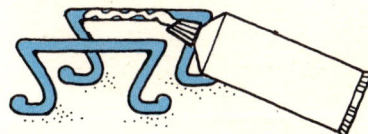

Cut 2 covered corrugated cardboard rectangles for lid. Make handle from 2 cardboard shapes glued together. Paint handle grey.

Cut 4 slits in 1 lid. Loop 2 plastic strips over handle and through slits. Glue ends at back. Glue the 2 lids together. Paint lid and box brown.

Cut grey paper strips. Glue them over corners and edges.

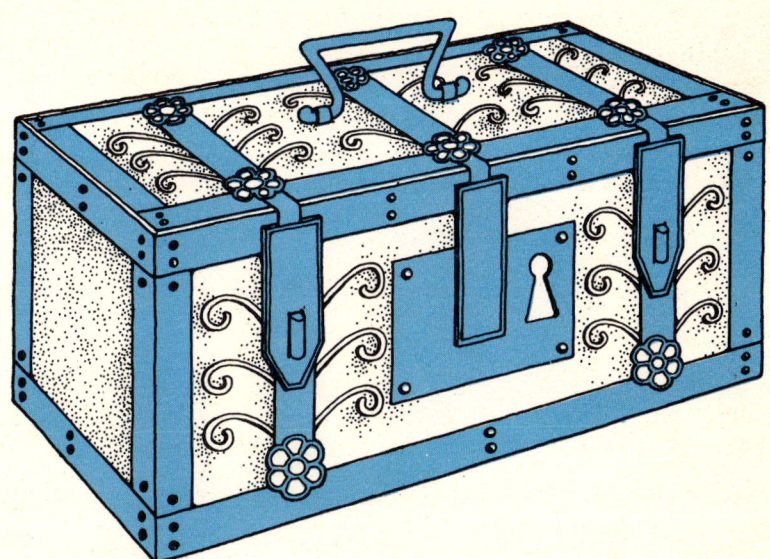

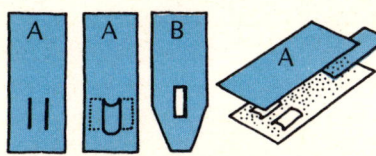

Cut 2 cardboard shapes for middle lock A. Make them ½ height of box. Cut 2 slits in 1 shape. Loop plastic strip, push ends through slits and glue in place. Glue a plastic strip between cardboard shapes at top.

Make 2 locks B same height as A from 4 cardboard shapes. Glue plastic strips between shapes at top. Cut out small holes.

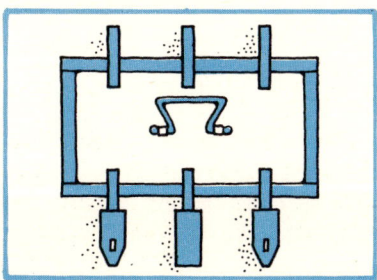

Glue locks and 3 plastic hinges on lid. Fit lid on box. Glue on hinges.

Cut metal fittings from grey paper. Glue 3 on lid and back, and 2 on front. Cut rectangular lock for box front.

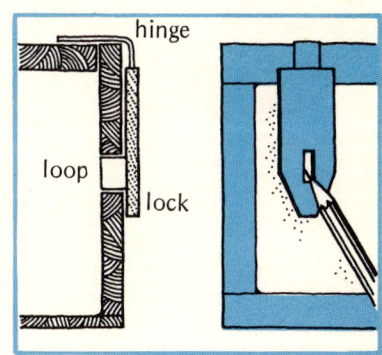

Fold middle lock down onto box front. Mark position of plastic loop. Cut hole so that loop fits snugly into box front. Mark position of holes in other locks. Cut slits in box front. Push 2 looped plastic strips through slits. Glue ends onto box. Paint some split peas grey. Glue them onto box as rivets. Paint on decorative patterns.

A KNIGHT'S SPURS

In the Middle Ages the greatest honour for a young man was to become a knight. Young noblemen were trained from the age of seven to fight with swords and lances, to hunt with falcons and bows and arrows, and to follow all the rules of chivalry. After years of training they were given their spurs as a sign that they were true knights.

The spurs were made of iron and were fastened to the boots with leather straps. The spiked wheels were used to urge the horse to move at a faster pace. Although an ordinary blacksmith could make a pair of spurs, few knights would have been satisfied with what he produced. Medieval knights took great pride in their spurs. Many pairs of spurs were elaborately decorated, and some were plated with silver.

How to make the spurs

Materials: wire, leather strips or plastic detergent bottle, kitchen foil, cardboard, paper fasteners, pencil, ruler, scissors, glue, paint, paintbrush

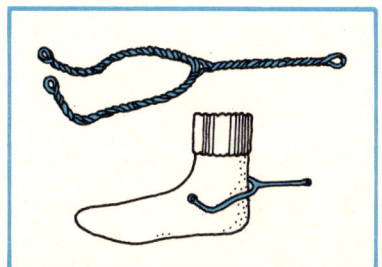

Twist several lengths of wire together to make basic spur shape that will fit your foot. Make loops at ends.

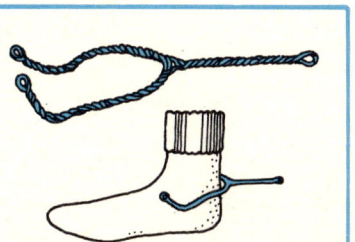

Cover frame with strips of kitchen foil.

Cut 6-pointed star from 5cm cardboard square. Cover both sides of star with kitchen foil.

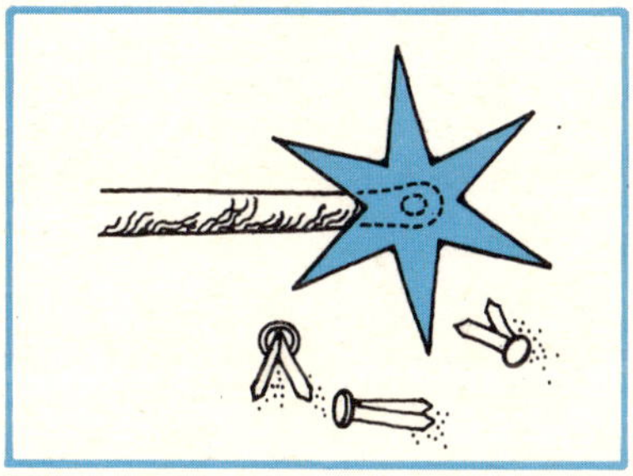

Make hole in centre of star and attach it to spur with paper fastener.

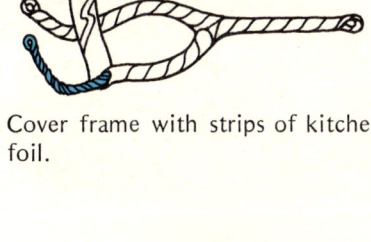

plastic strip

Make straps for spur from strips of leather. If leather is not available, use strips of plastic cut from a detergent bottle. Paint plastic brown.

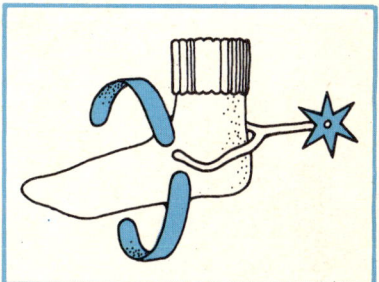

Cut 2 straps 1.5cm wide—1 to go over and 1 to go under your foot.

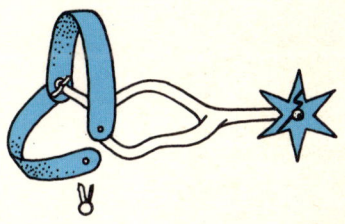

Make holes in strap ends. Attach straps to spur with paper fasteners. Make another spur to to complete the pair.

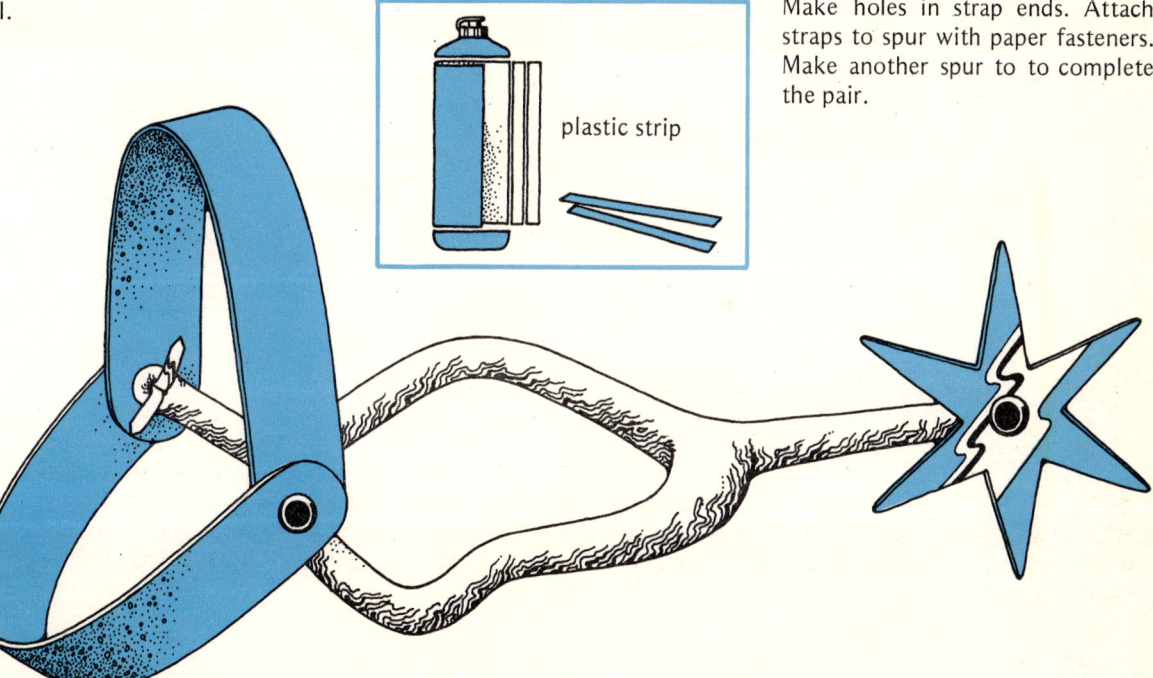

31

First published in Great Britain 1978 by Owlet Books, Mills & Boon
Limited, 17-19 Foley Street, London W1A 1DR.

Owlet Books
© Mills & Boon Ltd 1978

All rights reserved. No part of this publication may
be reproduced, stored in a retrieval system, or transmitted
in any form or by any means, electronic, mechanical,
photocopying, recording or otherwise, without the prior
permission of Mills & Boon.

THE MIDDLE AGES   ISBN 0 263 06338 0

Printed in Italy